AF316648

Ebb of Time

Ebb of Time

Joshua Jorgensen

CONTENTS

One

Love Contrasts

Time shifts each era in the stomach of the cosmos, digesting everything in the acids of entropy. So, ready your fate cause none will wait for what's at stake is the flesh to drip off fresh. Voice your tremble and pitch, a perishable plea. Slowly dispersing breath, a count down to pressure panic love.

Contraire to time's tendency to loosen allure and wilt. Then what's left is mine beautiful confined. Inquiring eyes will look inside but beware the enemy, I witnessed and caused my dread. Cannot impede settling seeds of death. Look what snuffed the precious breath, once loved now dead.

Contest this rot surrounding me, and bane is what remains. Hold dearly apart my heart and announce egress each beat decay. And fears will proof my reach a fake, because fears tightens life entangling me entwines pulling far from yond my sight.

Silent prayers are tears in speech. O' Spirit of Peace, you paid these fees, death a curse from the first meant to be. Let go of strife and now I'm free. Learned to Love not from me, this chance to change myself for Truth.

Garden

My heart's day of rain perfects this song I sing. A downpour across these fields no more barren and now deluge. Falls each drop into church ensembled rainfall. The flowing waters pools an embodied selfless nature. Purpose for replenish life for all and any find delight.

But beware the trust in dictators, driven generations far from once a home. We were once a home with no walls, these times lost long ago. Worrisome narratives provoking deals buy two, now bought a lesser me. Objective joys taught lies first infects the mind and the wages are repose. More is a monster who steals voices and what remains is less a heart. Monsters bearing names in primal origin, string perverse and scheme.

The silent requests are solace and rest. So, are the peaceable abide in vines reaching without eyes to grow. How hope extends a soul in song, could then words spark the Spirit reverbing as sounds array. Might I honor to have each breath believe the light to gift a warmth and serve alike the rays of sun. Teach my mean to shine, sow your seed who's found.

Truly good will not end. The path you lead, your Light I follow.

Two

Light My Path

Memories

Wheresoever I go, immersive memories last. Refuse myself a devouring past, never-ending hunger of times alas. And alas my collective is a lens perspective. A focus curved in stirred with malice. Plea I flee my mind's ingress, this mask is worn now frowns too fast. I ask what should I seem appear, my memories are fraught with rue dismay. I wither and shrivel in shadow my pain. Unbearable fates, are the plights my sickness makes. Deep are my roots, I'm lost in darkness. Which way is life? I fight for each breathe raught shallow and tight.

I pray for hope having colors compliment each other, inspire conversing from within the heart. A stillness quiet preludes a song of insight singing symphonies, "You shall not faulter focus for bright is my Light. Persevere and blossom beyond traced fright. Mustering growth, never sever upright. Whereby each petal unfolds a framework inlay bloomed perfect in sound and sight. Your best has yet will soon take flight."

Hope now reveals me wholly resolute and memories no longer abide me sold.

Pebble

Prayer perfects my joys. Then better I'll be when meaning gives perceived, I'll sought to spare a care. As do wisdom walks above the world of wants, displacing weight for thanks and font.

Could hope be the size of a pebble, dense in possibility ergo indefinite value. Forgo of any trade cause loss will give a cost. This pebble calling for caliber, all is bold whom hold. Having one, two could follow lest a fraught and loss by phantom. When one speaks truth heard by one, then two could not have fathomed. Beyond my eyes and touch proclaims, perfect is one profound in hitori.

Truth is beauty worthy for one. Aware the frail naïve as youth has shown, destructive qualms blinds eyes who trust on loan. Amid the dire of fire obscene, be close my pebble our faith holds us together.

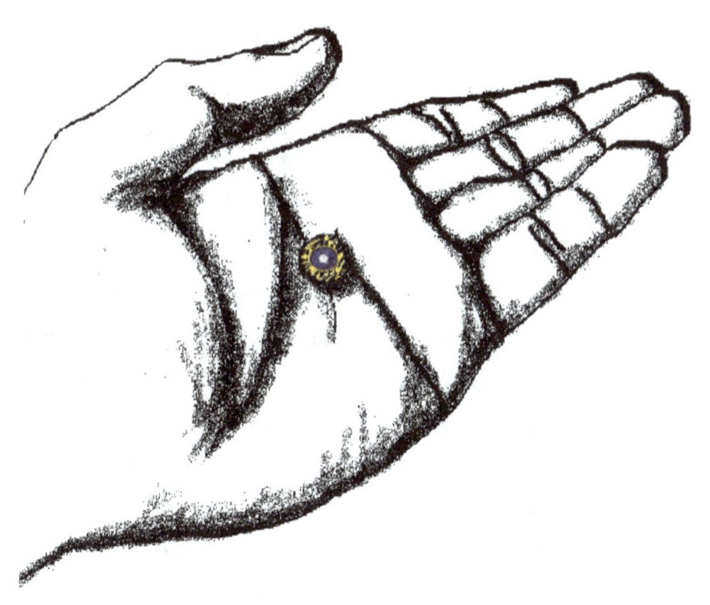

Time

Time descants rhythmic symphony ensembles. Confined to cause impending flaws but hope convicts made flesh symbolic. We're born with a gem, safe inside but the world forsakes. Each gem rests within till each their end or one undo. Rebuke who scoffs their names are Faust. Each step will stride towards fate. Pulled by strings impending scenes if choice all dies and never dream.

Tidings are for follow and silence adheres, objective the mind finds times fallible binds. What bends between unknown foreseen, so sow your night by day will change. A Love certain unseen from bane, outside of time two hearts combine. Pride is bound to shame confound. Kindness shapes in selfless hands, reveals a Hope sealed from sight. Whence moments come less and lesser nigh comes say, "Protect your gem and words of Hope, you'll never fall short hence forth good wealth."

Binary

The will made spoken ponders spells yet seen. Spells are from the spirit speaking letters, feeding readers soothing caters or raping seether. Layer a thick intent lest be the one possessed and plagued in mind. Suffering scenes embodies fiends, inching closer towards the ends each hold. Cause the mind's insight borderlines the surface outside. Receives receipts the soul has seized folding in on everyone else but mine.

The world weighs truth as binary, never counting two. Reluctant to share my dreams has caused me held and bound, "Unlikely" once said. Then give me lists of disposition, my character with a name. Tell me who I am before I do, if fate was spite. Then piece your temp to me as if Truth is meant to be spent, my adherence will not pledge devotion. Say your sight to see for me, you forget hope draws from honesty. Before farewell I'll ask to trade for Truth, I hope you'll say "No." You see the compounds of my chemicals, the demise to deterior. Should the upmost stability be faith, then prescription's no fine.

Prescription Receipt

01100110 01100001 01101001 01110100 01101000

Cost: $0.00

Three

Faith Reveal

Patience

In each physical domain is a limitless inlay coalescing harmony. Exceeding sights far stretched across wild expanse. No treasure any longer remembered could amount to the blood born from war. Every genus will craft from mishaps shifting the eras we share. But beware for versed societal indignancy decreed, casting offsets in forth honesty.

Though the molds of my insides nigh be seen, au contraire art would I rather hope be me. But even objective piety shall not withstand to Judgment, so leave what's left lacks or on lien. The war started is unseen and our soul is the anadem at hand. And no fate will be left yet faced. Come now liberate with Truth, a shout or silence O' Holy Spirit inspire. Patience reveals this moment clear. Holy Spirit come show us Love has won!

Hearken, there up high in the clouds! Our Lord Christ Jesus far exceeds all power! Angels beset us a heavenly host, Seraphs amass Cherubs Holy and chaste! How great the multi encompassed from Heaven! Christ Lord redeems us, by Grace and tempered Faith!

Hallelujah, God's Word is Christ Lord and none higher!

Greater the afflicter decides the victor. Learned to fight for itself because the world fights itself. But who will protect when the world does not protect? Does not know who to protect when wars against ourselves. Corruption covers intent thick in lies, knows greater threats are from within the lines. Worst deeds are wicked holds dominions by man. Weaponizing mind holds hostage hearts. Scheming deceit confiding to tongue and tone. Pervasive sermons exalts the self for servitude, enacting sleeping souls to bind. Those amok heralds death as thrones. Has eyes but sees no sorrow in sight, set their paths for waste and wrath. Evil defined to spread its kind, multiplies evil once met by evil.

Great weight are the wars of men, times when laws lost and minds will bend. Whence revelation signs fruition, Christ Jesus our righteous returns. Our suffer will cease, the Lord's grace all feast! Faith is a feather as family flocks together, will be our severance from forsaken. Greater gifts are given to each.

By Christ we live with Love we sing. Reigns the Lord's peace unyielding, everlasting God's season!